Farm Tractors

Andrew Morland

Motorbooks International
Publishers & Wholesalers

Acknowledgments

Thank you to all the enthusiastic owners of classic farm tractors in America and Canada, whose help and cooperation made this book possible.

Special thanks to the following for allowing me to take photographs on their sites: Roger Mohr Collection, Vail, Iowa; The Two-Cylinder Club and the John Deere Historic Site at Grand Detour, Dixon, Illinois; and the Ontario Agricultural Museum, Milton, Canada. Thanks also to the Keller family of Forest Junction, Wisconsin, for allowing me to photograph their rare John Deere tractors.

For information on tractor events in the United States and Canada, I recommend the Steam and Gas Show Directory, printed annually by Stemgas Publishing Company, PO Box 328, Lancaster, Pennsylvania 17603.

First published in 1993 by Motorbooks International Publishers & Wholesalers, PO Box 2, 729 Prospect Avenue, Osceola, WI 54020 USA

© Andrew Morland, 1993

Motorbooks International books are also available at discounts in bulk quantity for industrial or sales-promotional use. For details write to Special Sales Manager at the Publisher's address

Printed and bound in Hong Kong

Library of Congress Cataloging-in-Publication Data

Morland, Andrew.
    Farm tractors / Andrew Morland.
        p.   cm. — (Enthusiast color series)
    Includes index.
    ISBN 0-87938-824-2
    1. Farm tractors—History. I. Title. II. Series.
TL233.M567 1993
629.225—dc20   93-17026

On the front cover: Oliver introduced its streamlined Fleetline Series of farm tractors in 1948, including this stylish Row Crop 66.

On the back cover: The year 1934 witnessed the debut of John Deere's new general-purpose row-crop model, the Model A. This 1934 A featured an open fan shaft. The owner of this early A is Jim Quinn of East Peoria, Illinois.

On the frontispiece: The Massey-Harris No 2. tractor was powered by the smooth four-cylinder Buda engine, mounted crossways on top of the 7in steel tractor chassis. Initially rated as a 12–25 horsepower, the last models were down rated to 12 horsepower and 22 horsepower at 1000rpm.

On the title page: This Minneapolis-Moline RTI Military model was built in 1952 and was typical of the RTI models used by the US Air Force during the Korean War. The four-cylinder engine created 24 horsepower. This RTI is owned by Roger Mohr.

Contents

Chapter 1

International Harvester Tractors

The International Red Farmall Farms All

In 1906, the International Harvester Company of Chicago created its first tractor, which eventually evolved into the famous Farmall.

The Farmall became the quintessential tractor, the one by which all others were judged. It was designed with the small farmer in mind; brought "power farming" within reach of farmers throughout the United States and Canada due to its small size and small price.

The roots of the International Harvester Company stretch back to the mid-1800s when Cyrus Hall McCormick created his first reaper. McCormick's chief competition in the field came from the Deering family, but faced with tough times in the farming marketplace, the Deerings offered a merger. On August 12, 1902, the International Harvester Company was born.

Alongside its Farmall tractor, IH offered a broad range of farm machinery from threshers to combines, disks to plows. In the late 1970s, the United Automobile Workers (UAW) struck IH, and along with the depressed farm economy, forced International to cut back. In the mid-1980s, IH was acquired by Tenneco, which also owned Case.

Opposite page
McCormick-Deering W-40
Built by the International Harvester Company between 1934 and 1940, production totalling 6,454. This six-cylinder gasoline engine produced 32 horsepower at the drawbar compared to the diesel's 37 horsepower.

International Harvester Farmall 300
The Farmall 300 model was introduced in 1954 as a three-plow, general-purpose row-crop tractor. It was powered by International Harvester's four-cylinder C-196 engine with a bore and stroke that measured 3.47x4.25in. The 300's short life span ended in 1956 after only two years of production.

McCormick-Deering W-30

The International Harvester Company, the W30 was built from 1932 to 1940 with more than 32,000 produced. The gasoline/kerosene engine developed 19.7 horsepower at the drawbar and 31.2 horsepower at the belt. The standard four-speed gearbox allowed a top speed of 4mph. The engine hood's side door has been removed to show the tall, long-stroke four-cylinder engine that was developed from the 15-30 model. Note the two hand-hole covers in the engine block for easy access.

Photographed on the Kurt Umnus Farm, Edgar, Wisconsin, during the North Central Steam and Gas Engine Show.

T he first steam ploughing engine is credited to J. W. Fawkes, and was built in 1858. It drew eight plows in prairie sod at the rate of three miles per hour.

—*Victor Pagé,* ***The Modern Gas Tractor,*** *1913*

International Harvester McCormick W-4
The W-4 was introduced in 1940 and continued in production all the way through to 1953. Designed as a standard-tread version of the Farmall H model, it also shared the H's four-cylinder, 152ci C-152 engine. The W-4 was designed with a cast-iron frame, five-speed gearbox, and independent braking system. The engine was rated at a full 24 horsepower. This W-4 was photographed in Great Britain where many W-4s, W-6s, and W-9s came under the World War II Lend-Lease agreements with the United States.

International Farmall Super M
The Super M featured an adjustable tread width
that could be stretched from 52in to 88in. This
superbly restored example is owned by the
Bunker family of Lena, Illinois.

International Harvester Farmall Super M

The Farmall M was introduced in 1939 and was built for twelve full years, reigning as one of the best known of all Farmalls. The gasoline-engined Super M, however, was only built from 1952 to 1953. The Super had the popular Torque Amplifier option, which was a lever-operated speed range control.

Right
International Farmall Super M

Details of the Super M four-cylinder gasoline engine; a diesel version was also available, designated as the MD. The Super M's five-speed gearbox gave a speed of 2–3mph in low gear and a top speed of 17mph in high.

Chapter 2

John Deere Tractors

The Waterloo Boy and Deere Green Poppin' Johnny

Deere and Company has grown from a small one-man blacksmith shop making steel plows to a giant international corporation. Along the way, the Deere family and the Deere company has had its hand in building everything from automobiles to snowmobiles, bicycles to airplanes. But it is the John Deere farm tractor, and its accompanying line of implements, that have made Deere the world's most famous agricultural equipment manufacturer.

Deere's entry into the tractor fold was belated when compared with the other American farm equipment makers. Deere was concentrating on the production of its plows and select other implements at the turn of the century and was not ready to get into the power farming field.

Deere began experimenting with tractors such as the Melvin, Dain, and Sklovsky tractors in the 1910s before purchasing the Waterloo Gasoline Engine Company of Waterloo, Iowa, in 1918. Waterloo built its own tractor, the Waterloo Boy, which was now added to the John Deere line.

When the Waterloo Boy grew outdated, Deere developed its own tractor, based largely on the Waterloo Boy. The Model D made its debut in 1924, followed by the famous line of two-cylinder general-purpose row-crop tractors. From 1934 to

Opposite page
John Deere Model B
The Model B was the quintessential Poppin' Johnny two-cylinder general-purpose row-crop John Deere tractor. Introduced in 1935, this particular tractor is serial number B1000, the very first Model B produced. In all, more than 300,000 Model Bs were sold, marking this as John Deere's best-selling tractor. This historic Model B belongs to the Keller family of Forest Junction, Wisconsin.

1960, these "Poppin' Johnnies" built the Deere legend.

In 1960, Deere introduced its new, modern line of four-cylinder tractors, still painted in the famous Deere Green with yellow trim. And Deere continues into the 1990s with a full line of two- and four-wheel-drive tractors, combines, and implements.

Waterloo Boy Model R
Detail of the gorgeous Waterloo Boy emblem that highlights the fuel tank of the Model R.

Top
Waterloo Boy Model R
The Waterloo Gasoline Engine Company of Waterloo, Iowa, built the Waterloo Boy tractor, which garnered such a strong reputation that Deere and Company bought out the whole company. The Model R was built from 1914 to 1919. The 465ci two-cylinder engine had a bore and stroke measuring 6.50x7.00in and was rated at 16 horsepower at the drawbar. The owner of this beautifully restored Model R is Tony Ridgeway of West Unity, Ohio.

John Deere Model A
The year 1934 witnessed the debut of John Deere's new general-purpose row-crop models, including the Model A. This 1934 A featured an open fan shaft, which can be seen rotating on the engine. The owner of this early A is Jim Quinn of East Peoria, Illinois.

John Deere Model B
The University of Nebraska Tractor Tests rated the Model B general-purpose row-crop tractor at 9.28 drawbar horsepower and 14.25 belt horsepower.

Left
John Deere Model A
The Model A was a general-purpose row-crop tractor built from 1934 to 1952 and designed to fill in the John Deere line between the three-plow Model D and the one-plow Model GP; thus, the Model A could pull two plows. This early, unstyled A was powered by Deere's famous two-cylinder 309ci engine, which was rated at 16.22 drawbar horsepower and 23.52 belt horsepower at the University of Nebraska Tractor Tests. More than 300,000 units were built during its production run, in several variations, which included the AN single front-wheel model; AW adjustable-axle, wide front model; ANH and AWH Hi-Crop versions; AR standard-tread, non-row-crop model; AO orchard tractor; and the streamlined AOS. This A is owned by the Keller family of Forest Junction, Wisconsin.

J ohn Deere, the man, is gone. But the simple pride that John Deere felt in every plow that bore his name is the ruling pride of the makers of John Deere quality equipment today.

—Deere and Company brochure, 1937

Following pages
John Deere Model BWH
After creating the Model D as a replacement for the Waterloo Boy, Deere engineers turned their hands to designing a general-purpose tractor that small farmers could afford to own and operate. After building several experimental prototypes, Deere released a limited run of its new row-crop tractor, called the Model C, which was soon refined and renamed the GP, for general-purpose. The Model B replaced the GP in 1935 and was powered by a two-cylinder 149ci engine with 4.25in bore and 5.25in stroke backed by a four-speed gearbox. The BWH was a Model B Hi-Crop variation with an adjustable, wide-tread front axle. This very collectible unstyled Deere is owned by the Keller family of Forest Junction, Wisconsin.

John Deere Model 80 Diesel
Six years after its introduction, the diesel Model R was replaced by the Model 80. Built from 1955 to 1956, the 80 was rated at 61.8 horsepower at the drawbar. The two-cylinder diesel of 472ci was started by a gasoline, V-4 pony starter engine of 18.8ci. In 1956, the 80 was retired and the 820 took over its chores.

Right
John Deere Model BWH
The wide-tread stance of the Model BWH is obvious in this view. The University of Nebraska Tractor Tests rated this first-generation 149ci engine at 11.8 drawbar horsepower and 16 belt horsepower.

John Deere Model 70

The Model 70 arrived in 1953 as the Model G's successor, designed as a tough, strong tractor that was born to pull. This 70 featured a diesel engine backed with power steering. The two-cylinder diesel was the smallest of the 70-series engines, but produced 45.7 drawbar horsepower from its 376ci. A V-4 cylinder gasoline pony engine of 18.8ci was used as a starter for Deere's first diesel row-crop tractor. Production of the Model 70 series lasted from 1953–1956, when it was replaced by the new Model 720 series. This 70 is owned by Richard Rammange of Morrisonville, Wisconsin.

John Deere Model 70 Hi-Crop

The Model 70 was the replacement for the illustrious Model G, John Deere's three-plow general-purpose tractor. This Hi-Crop version of the 70 now stood in for the old GH Hi-Crop. This 70 featured power steering and the engine could run on LP-gas. The 379.5ci two-cylinder LPG was rated at 46.1 horsepower at the drawbar. Built from 1953–1956, it came with six forward gears and one reverse. This very collectible 70 was one of only twenty-five built, and is owned by Norman Smith of Carrollton, Illinois.

Left

John Deere Model 60 Row Crop

The Model 60 series replaced the grand old Model A in 1952. Its two-cylinder engine of 321ci was rated at 36.9 horsepower at the drawbar. The Model 60 was built until 1956, at which time it was retired and the Model 620 took its place. This Model 60 is owned by Richard Rammange of Morrisonville, Wisconsin.

John Deere Model 320

The Model 320 arrived in the nation's fields in 1956 as a new model derived from the original Model H and M. The 320 was designed especially for the small farmer and vegetable grower, and came in two versions, the 320S, or Standard, and the 320U, or Utility. The 320 was powered by a two-cylinder, 22.4 horsepower gasoline engine of 100.5ci. This 320 was photographed at the Two-Cylinder Club's show in the John Deere Historic Site at Grand Detour, Dixon, Illinois.

Chapter 3

J. I. Case Tractors

The Old Abe Mascot and Flambeau Red Tractors

Jerome Increase Case founded his J. I. Case Threshing Machine Company in Rochester, Wisconsin, in 1842. The firm's first creation was groundhog-type thresher; within a short time Case had graduated to building steam-engine-powered traction engines that were mamoth in size and power. In 1847, Case moved his firm to Racine, Wisconsin.

In 1876, Jerome Increase Case started a separate company with no ties to the threshing machine maker. This second firm, J. I Case Plow Works, was founded in Racine to offer plows; it was eventually controlled by the Wallis Tractor Company before being sold to the Canadian Massey-Harris firm in the 1920s. In 1928, Massey sold the rights to the Case name back to J. I. Case Threshing Machine Company.

Production of gasoline-powered tractors had started in the 1910s at the threshing machine firm as the demand for steam declined. The Models 30-60, 20-40, 12-25, and the four-cylinder 10-20 were offered beginning in 1912. In 1916, Case developed its Crossmotor models before moving on to standard and row-crop tractors in 1929. In the late 1930s, Case first painted its tractors its telltale Flambeau Red color.

In the late 1960s, Case was taken over by Tenneco, which continues to manufacture Case and International Harvester tractors in the 1990s.

Opposite page
Case R
This Case R, built in 1938, was powered by the L-head, four-cylinder Waukesha engine that measured 3.25in bore and 4.00in stroke. Rated at 16 horsepower at the drawbar and 19.25 horsepower at the belt, the R Series led the way for Case up until World War II. This R is owned by Betty and Lee Norton of Alto, Michigan.

Case Crossmotor 15-27
Close-up of the clutch and magneto on the
Crossmotor. The hand-operated, twin-disk clutch
was fitted inside the belt pulley. Case did not
change to foot-operated clutches until 1955.

Left
Case Crossmotor 15-27
The J. I. Case Crossmotor 15-27 was first
offered in 1919 with production continuing
through 1924. It produced 27 horsepower on the
belt and 15 horsepower on the drawbar. At a
maximum engine speed of 900rpm,
33 horsepower was available, giving a top speed
of 3mph. The four-cylinder 381ci engine had a
4.50in bore and 6.00in stroke. At 6,350 pounds
the 15-27 was no lightweight. This 15-27 was
photographed in the early morning sun with its
correct LC Gray color and Case Red pinstripes.
It is owned by Bill Kuhn of Kinde, Michigan.

Case Crossmotor 15-27
The essential features of the Case Crossmotor tractor series included a cross-mounted, vertical four-cylinder engine with 4.50in bore and 6.00in stroke; a three-bearing crankshaft; renewable cylinder sleeves; exhaust-heated intake manifold; water air cleaner; water-feed valve carburetor; twin-disk clutch fitted inside the belt pulley; cast-iron frame; and fully enclosed, all spur gear, two-speed transmission, and final drives. The 15-27 was basically the same tractor as the 18-32, differing in horsepower output due to engine modifications.

Case Crossmotor 10-18

In the mid-1910s, tractor manufacturers began to focus on building tractors designed to handle two-, three-, and four-bottom plows. In 1916, J. I. Case introduced its Crossmotor Model 9-18, a lightweight, streamlined, two-plow tractor. In 1918–1919, Case boosted the 9-18's horsepower output by increasing engine rpm and redesignated it the Model 10-18. The 10-18 was tested at the University of Nebraska in April 1920, where its engine developed 18.41 belt horsepower and 11.24 drawbar horsepower.

Maximum drawbar pull was measured at 1,730 pounds. A new feature of the 10-18 was Case's patented Air Washer, which drew outside air into a canister then through water that trapped dirt particles. A screen then filtered out the dust and clean air continued through the system into the carburetor. The 10-18 was offered in both agricultural and industrial models. This 1919 Crossmotor 10-18 was photographed with owner and restorer John David of Maplewood, Ohio, at the controls.

Case R

By the 1920s, Case's Crossmotor tractors were outdated. The Fordson and International Farmall had arrived on the scene and were taking away much of Case's small-farmer tractor market. The Fordson and Farmall offered the advantages of a unitized chassis design, which made for a lighter tractor. In 1930, Case responded with its general-purpose R Series tractors.

Left

Case DCS Sugar Cane Special

J. I. Case's D Series tractors replaced the old C Series in 1939, offering new styling that was dressed up in Case's new corporate Flambeau Red paint scheme. Through the series run, Case offered a number of variations on the basic D including this rare DCS Sugar Cane Special with its high stance. Built in 1952, this DCS was powered by a Case-built four-cylinder engine. When production of the D Series ended in 1953, more than 100,000 units had been built. This very collectible special is owned by Tom Graverson in Indiana.

Case D

J. I. Case's D Series of tractors were built in many variations, including row-crop, industrial, orchard, and vineyard models. The standard Model D tractor,equipped with rubber tires and the new four-speed transmission, was tested at the University of Nebraska in June 1940. Fueled by distillate, engine output was measured at 31.87 brake horsepower and 24.86 drawbar horsepower. Model Ds were produced from 1939 to 1955; this D was built in 1950.

Right
Case VAH

In 1941, Case retired its V Series tractors and the VA Series bowed with a new Case-designed and -built engine to replace the Continental unit used in the V Series. Built in 1948, this VAH high-clearance tractor used the four-cylinder, 23 horsepower engine to work the cotton and tobacco fields of Kentucky.

Chapter 4

Minneapolis-Moline Tractors

The Prairie Gold Minne-Mo

The history of American farm equipment manufacturers is a history of corporate mergers. Firms struggled to stay alive in the fast-growing and rapidly changing marketplace after the turn of the century, and one way to build a strong company with a complete line of farming tools was to merge several firms into one.

Minneapolis-Moline Company of Minneapolis, Minnesota, was formed in 1929 by the merger of Minneapolis Steel & Machinery Company of Minneapolis, the Moline Implement Company of Moline, Illinois, and the Minneapolis Threshing Machine Company of Hopkins, Minnesota.

With this combined force, the new company was able to offer farmers a full line of equipment including the famous Twin City tractors, Minneapolis threshers, and a variety of implements, grain drills, wagons, and tillage tools.

"Minne-Mo" became one of the stalwart American tractor manufacturers of the 1930s and postwar years. Its Prairie Gold-painted tractors were easily identified against the green of fields, and farmers came to rely on the power and dependability of the tractors and equipment.

Minneapolis-Moline became part of the White Farm Equipment in 1963, joining Oliver and Cockshutt. In 1972, production was transferred from Minneapolis, Minnesota, to Charles City, Iowa. In 1974, the MM name was dropped from tractors and replaced by the White name.

Minneapolis-Moline RTU

Minne-Mo's R Series tractors made their debut in 1939 with the RT model; by 1940, four versions were available, including the RTN, RTI, RTS, and RTU. Tested by the University of Nebraska in 1940, it was rated at 20–24 horsepower at 1400rpm. This RTU model was built in 1949.

The Minneapolis-Moline merger of 1929 brought together three companies that, if they had remained independent, probably would not have survived the Grea Depression.

—*C. H. Wendel,*
***Minneapolis-Moline Tractors**, 1990*

Twin City 21-32

The Twin City line of tractors was inherited by Minneapolis-Moline in the three-part merger that formed the company in 1929. Twin City tractors had been built by the Minneapolis Steel & Machinery Company, and continued in production under the Twin City name as the line was so well known and respected among farmers. This 21-32 tractor was built in 1930.

Far left
Minneapolis-Moline UDLX
The UDLX Comfortractor was some thirty years ahead of its time, and many farmers chose the more-traditional open-cab Model U tractor over the UDLX. Because of its avant-garde design and high cost of $2,155, only about 150 were sold during its production run of 1938–1941. This 1938 UDLX is part of the Roger Mohr collection.

Minneapolis-Moline UDLX
The Comfortractor shared its engine with the Model U. With 40–45 horsepower on tap, top speed was 40mph. With its five-speed gearbox and foot throttle, the UDLX was designed to plow all day and then be driven downtown in the evening—a combination car and tractor for the modern farmer of the 1930s!

Twin City 21-32
The 21-32 model made its debut in 1930 and was offered by Minneapolis-Moline through 1934, still wearing the Twin City nameplate. The 21-32 was a successful model, pulling three to four plow bottoms. This tractor was beautifully restored by Leo Andea of Dryden, Michigan, and was photographed at the Mid-Iowa Antique Power Association meet at Marshalltown, Iowa, where it won Best of Show honors.

Minneapolis-Moline UDLX

The Comfortractor was designed with safety and weather protection in mind. The insulated, impact-resistant cab featured safety glass, windshield wipers, radio, heater, and hot-air defrosting—all the comforts of a car, including an easy-change five-speed gearbox and foot throttle. As with many advanced designs, the UDLX attracted few customers in its day, though, today, it is one of the most collectible MMs.

Minneapolis-Moline GTA
This GTA of 1946 was designed to pull a four- to five-plow load. The engine was a four-cylinder of 403.2ci with paired blocks. The bore and stroke measured 4.625x6.00in. Backed by a four-speed gearbox and rated at 49 horsepower, the engine produced a maximum belt power of 55 horse-power. All engines came standard with force-fed lubrication and a balanced camshaft for smooth running. This massive engine alone weighs more than one ton. The GTA sported a yellow grille whereas the early GT had a red grille. This GTA is from the Roger Mohr collection.

Left
Minneapolis-Moline RTU
The four-cylinder engine of the 1949 RTU was rated at 20–24 horsepower at 1400 rpm. The engine had a 3.625in bore and 4.00in stroke with unusually long rocker arms and horizontal valves. Only two main bearings held the crankshaft, but the front was an extra-strong roller bearing. Overall, the engine design was a great success, offering ease of maintenance and a long life. The owner of this RTU is Jim Adams of Marshalltown, Iowa.

Minneapolis-Moline M5
By the 1960s, Minneapolis-Moline production was centered at White Farm Equipment's Hopkins, Minnesota, plant. This M5 tractor from 1960 was typical of the new generation of White-built Minne-Mos. The four-cylinder engine displaced with a 4.625in bore and 5.00in stroke. Power steering was standard. This M5 is from the Roger Mohr collection.

Following pages
Minneapolis-Moline Four Star 1961.
Production of the Four Star ran from 1959 to 1964; this tractor dates from 1961. The Four Star's gasoline engine was rated at 44.57 PTO horsepower, but it was also available in diesel or LP-gas configuration. This Four Star is from the Roger Mohr collection.

Chapter 5

Massey Tractors

The Pride of Canada

The Massey-Harris Company was the result of a merger in 1891 of two stalwart Canadian agricultural firms, Massey Manufacturing Company of Toronto, Ontario, and A. Harris, Son & Company of Brantford, Ontario.

Massey-Harris made its debut in the tractor market in 1917 with the Bull tractor built by the Bull Tractor Company of Minneapolis, Minnesota, which later became the Toro Company. By 1918, Massey-Harris was building its own tractor, the MH-1, based on a design by the Parrett Tractor Company of Chicago.

Massey-Harris continued to build a wide range of row-crop general-purpose tractors but the firm's product was refined in the mid-1950s when it merged with Harry Ferguson, Incorporated. Ferguson had developed the three-point hitch and draft control that revolutionized Henry Ford's N Series of tractors; with this merger, Massey-Ferguson was formed, and a new line of models was created.

Opposite page
Massey-Harris 81 R
Massey-Harris built its 81 R standard-tread tractor from 1941–1946, during which time it was used extensively by the Royal Canadian Air Force. In 1946, production switched to row-crop style 81 Rs, which continued through to 1948. This 81 R was built in 1942, and bears serial number 425727. This tractor is owned by Diane Fisher of Milton, Ontario.

Massey-Harris No. 2

The Massey-Harris No. 2 tractor was built under license through a deal with the Parrett Tractor Company of Chicago. This particular tractor was built circa 1921 at Massey-Harris' Weston factory on the outskirts of Toronto, Ontario. Its large-diameter front wheels were designed by Dent and Henry Parrett to minimize soil compaction and reduce bearing wear by moving the hubs further from the soil. The Massey-Harris No. 2 was rated as a 12–25 horsepower tractor, and sold well in the boom period following World War I. This No. 2 is owned by the Ontario Agriculture Museum.

Left

Massey-Harris Pony

The Massey-Harris Pony was the firm's smallest tractor, rated at 16–27 horsepower and designed for the small farmer or vegetable grower. First offered in 1947, production continued through to 1952 with a last batch built in 1957. Power came from a four-cylinder Continental engine. This Pony was manufactured in 1951, and came complete with hydraulic lift. The Pony pictured is owned by Larry Darling of Michigan.

Massey-Harris No. 3

The No. 3 was a refinement of the Parrett-designed No. 2. Despite repositioning the radiator to update the look, the No. 3 still had a strange stance. The front axle had to remain far forward, however, to retain the steering lock required by the large-diameter front wheels. The No. 3 was now rated at 15–28 horsepower.

Massey-Harris No. 3

The horsepower increase to 28 on the belt at 1000rpm was derived from the enlarged Massey-Harris No. 2 Buda engine. Bore was now at 4.50in with a 6.50in stroke. But even the power increase failed to sell the tractor in the highly competitive agricultural market. In 1923, the year this tractor was built, production stopped at the Weston factory. This No. 3 is owned by the Ontario Agricultural Museum.

Left

Massey-Harris Model No. 3

The four-cylinder Buda engine was mounted transversely in the No. 3's frame. The fan belt drive turned 90 degrees to run the oil and magneto shaft and allow for easy access. Crank starting was on the right side of the engine with pulley power take-off on the other side.

55

A griculture is the basis of any country's prosperity. It is the most important of the occupations of man because it furnishes the majority of the foodstuffs that sustain life.

*—Victor Pagé, **The Modern Gas Tractor**, 1913*

Massey-Harris 102GS Junior Twin-Power
The 102 Series Massey-Harris's were popular tractors of the late 1930s and 1940s. This 102GS Junior had the added benefit of Twin-Power, which offered a range of different governor settings over the standard Junior. Built in 1945, this 102GS boasted 25 horsepower. This tractor is owned by Ivan Henderson of Cambridge, Ontario.

Following pages
Massey-Harris Pony
Built in 1949, at the Woodstock factory in Canada, the Pony was Massey-Harris' smallest model. The 62ci Continental four-cylinder engine of the Pony had a bore of 2.375in and a stroke of 3.50in. The Pony was rated as a 10 horsepower or one-plow tractor. This Pony is owned by Bill Kuhn of Kinde, Michigan.

Left

Massey-Harris 81 R

The 81 R was a popular wartime model, and many were bought by the Royal Canadian Air Force for towing aircraft. In RCAF guise, the tractors were painted in camouflage, not Massey-Harris' trademark red.

Massey-Harris 101 Super Row Crop

The 101 Super Row Crop was one of the most advanced and stylish Massey-Harris tractors. The streamlined bodywork completely enclosed the engine—an advanced design for its time. Today, the 101 Super with the Chrysler 35 horsepower six-cylinder engine is probably the most collectible of the Massey-Harris range of tractors. Many 101 Supers lost their pretty, vented side panels around the farm or in the fields, however. The later 1940–1944 Supers had more conventional half-enclosed panels and Continental, 26–40 horsepower side-valve engines. This 101 was built in 1939.

Chapter 6

Allis-Chalmers Tractors

The Persian Orange Tractors

Corporate mergers formed the shape of the farm tractor and equipment industry, but the Allis-Chalmers Company stands ahead of all the other manufacturers in the number of disparate companies that joined together over decades to form this one firm.

Allis-Chalmers' roots stretch back to 1847 when James Decker and Charles Seville formed a company to built flour-making tools; Edward P. Allis, one half of the Allis-Chalmers name, soon bought them out. In 1901, Allis joined with Fraser & Chalmers of Chicago, Dickson Manufacturing Company of Pennsylvania, and Gates Iron Works of Chicago to create Allis-Chalmers.

Allis had built steam engines as early as 1869, but the new company's first tractors were unveiled after the turn of the century. Allis-Chalmers continued to add other companies to its corporate rooster, including tractor builders such as the famous and long-lived Advance-Rumely line and the Monarch Tractor Corporation that constructed crawlers.

Opposite page
Allis-Chalmers D12
Allis-Chalmers' popular line of D Series tractors included both the D10 and D12 models, which differed only in their tread configurations. The D10 had a narrow tread and was designed for one-row cultivation; the D12 had a wide stance and was built for two-row work. This D12 was built in 1959 and bears serial number 1741.

Allis-Chalmers Model U
The Model U was one of Allis-Chalmers' most popular and best-selling tractor lines. Introduced in 1929, the Model U continued in production until 1952, by which time more than 20,000 units had been built. This U was manufactured in 1936. The four-cylinder Allis-Chalmers engine had a bore of 4.375in and a stroke of 5.00in. This engine produced 33.18 horsepower at the drawbar at 1200rpm in the University of Nebraska Tractor Tests. This U is owned by Alan Draper of Bishopstone, Salisbury, Great Britain.

Right
Allis-Chalmers WD45
The WD45 was introduced in 1955 with a six-cylinder 230ci engine rated at a brawny 40 brake horsepower. The WD45 created its power via a diesel engine based on the great Buda diesels (Allis-Chalmers had bought out the Buda Company in the early 1950s to gain this expertise). This 1956 WD45, owned by Theodore Buisker of Davis, Illinois, is still used every day for farming. Buisker first drove a WD45 at the tender age of five years.

Allis-Chalmers D19

The Allis-Chalmers D19 was only built for three years, from 1961–1963. A number of variations to the D19 were available, including gasoline, LP-gas, or diesel fuel models as well as an industrial version painted in utility yellow. This D19, bearing serial number 13149, was built in 1963 and is from the Larry and Edwin Karg collection.

Allis-Chalmers D17 Mk IV
The popular D17 Allis-Chalmers model was introduced in 1957 with updated models appearing over the next ten years. The Series II began production in 1959; the Series III in 1964; and the final Series IV in 1965. This D17 Series IV, built in 1966 and still going strong, is powering a Haybine hay cutter.

Left
Allis-Chalmers D12
The D12 was powered by a reliable four-cylinder engine with a 149ci displacement and a bore and stroke measuring 3.50x3.875in. This D12 was restored by Edwin Karg of Hutchinson, Minnesota, who, with his son Larry, spends most of his time restoring Allis-Chalmers D Series tractors.

Ford Tractors

The Ford Tractor With the Ferguson System

Henry Ford was born on a farm and when he set out to build a farm tractor, his goal was to ease the workload on the back of the nation's farmers by building a tractor comparable to his Model T automobile in simplicity and low cost.

Ford's first tractor experiments were based on Ford car chassis, which was not surprising as numerous other firms were offering kits to convert Model T cars into crude but effective farm tractors. In 1907, Ford unveiled his Automobile Plow based on a Model B car engine, but it remained a prototype until the famous—and infamous—Fordson tractor made its debut in 1917.

The Fordson earned praise and curses as one of the pioneer general-purpose tractors. With increased competition from International Harvester's Farmall, the Fordson ceased production int eh United States in 1928, although they conitnued to be built in Dagenham, England.

In 1939, Ford re-entered the tractor market with the Ford 9N, which was supplemented by the three-point hitch and draft control features created by Harry Ferguson. Ford's N Series of tractors were revolutionary for the time, continuing in production until the Handshake Agreement between Ford Motor Company and Ferguson went sour in the 1940s.

Opposite page
Ford 8N Funk Brothers V-8
The Funk Brothers aviation company of Coffeeville, Kansas, offered a conversion kit for the Ford N Series tractors that allowed a farmer to hot-rod his or her workhorse. The kit extended the tractor chassis slightly to fit an 8BA L-head Ford V-8 engine, producing a stump-pulling 100 horsepower. The conversion included longer tie and radius rods, a raised hood and grille, larger radiator, and gearbox adaptors. Palmer Fossum of Northfield, Minnesota, owns this rare beast.

Ford 9N with Ferguson System
The four-cylinder 120ci L-head Ford engine produced 28 horsepower at 2000rpm. The success of the 9N was due to its low price and the Ferguson System created by Irishman Harry Ferguson. The system's innovative, yet brilliantly simple three-point hitch and draft control revolutionized farm tractors.

Left
Ford 9N with Ferguson System
This Ford-Ferguson 9N tractor, serial number 357, is believed to be one of the oldest surviving 9Ns. Possibly built in the first week of production in 1939, it bears several imprints of the earliest N Series tractors. Note the horizontal grille and the early cast-aluminum hood; later 9Ns had vertical grilles and steel hoods. This tractor was restored by Ford collector Palmer Fossum of Northfield, Minnesota.

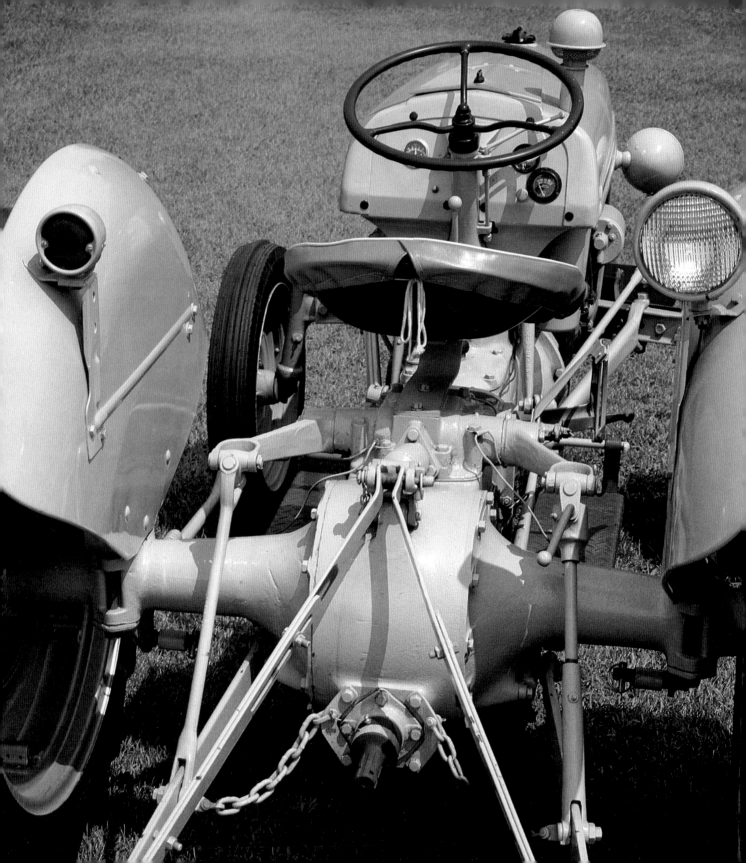

Ford 2N with Ferguson System

The Ford 2N replaced the original 9N in 1942, hence its "2" designation just as the earlier tractor bore the "9." From this view, the famous Ferguson System three-point hitch is clearly visible. Using hydraulic touch controls, the farmer could attach or detach implements without straining a muscle or wasting time. This 1946 2N is owned by Leroy Folkert.

Ford 501 Offset Workmaster

The Ford Motor Company and Harry Ferguson parted ways after a falling out over the Handshake Agreement between Ferguson and Henry Ford. Ferguson began building his own Ferguson tractors while Ford started its own line, including this 1958 501 Offset Workmaster. Designed for underframe-mounted tillage of sugar cane and vineyard farms, the 501 was powered by a four-cylinder 134ci Red Tiger engine with a four-speed gearbox. This 501 was restored and is owned by Palmer Fossum of Northfield, Minnesota.

Chapter 8

Oliver and Hart-Parr Tractors

The Company That Coined The Word "Tractor"

In 1897, Charles Hart and Charles Parr of Iowa combined forces to create the Hart-Parr Gasoline Engine Company in Madison, Wisconsin, although it soon moved to Charles City, Iowa. Hart-Parr built its first tractor in 1901 and coined the word "tractor" in 1906 to describe its self-propelled gasoline tractor and to replace the term that had been commonly used in the early days; gasoline traction engine. The company continued to produce some of the nation's largest and most powerful tractors through the early parts of the century.

In 1929, Hart-Parr merged with the Oliver Chilled Plow Company of South Bend, Indiana, Nichols & Shepard Company of Battle Creek, Michigan, and the American Seeding Machine Company of Springfield, Ohio, to become the Oliver Farm Equipment Company, based now in Chicago.

With this merger, the new firm offered a full line of tractors, tillage tools, and farm implements to battle the main marketplace forces of Deere and Company and International Harvester. From 1937 Hart-Parr was dropped from the name plate.

Together with Minneapolis-Moline and Cockshutt Plow Company of Brantford, Ontario, which sold Oliver tractors under its own name, Oliver became part of the White Motor Corporation in 1962.

Opposite page
Hart-Parr 12-24
In 1901, Charles Hart and Charles Parr joined forces to produce the stalwart Hart-Parr tractor series, finding a home in Charles City, Iowa. In 1929, Hart-Parr merged with the Oliver Chilled Plow Company and other firms, becoming the Oliver Corporation. Hart-Parr's 12-24 was a successful twin-cylinder tractor rated at 12 drawbar horsepower and 24 belt-pulley horsepower.

Oliver Row Crop

The Oliver Row Crop was a continuation of the
Hart-Parr 18-27 row-crop tractor. Built from
1937–1948, the Model 80 was powered by either
a gasoline or distillate engine. There was also an
80 Diesel model featuring a Buda-Lanova diesel
engine. This Row Crop model of the 1930s was
rated at 25–40 horsepower.

Right
Oliver Row Crop 77

In 1948, Oliver introduced its Fleetline Series of
tractors with modern styling and streamlined,
enclosed engines. The Row Crop 66, 77, and 88
models replaced the old 60, 70, and 80 tractors,
respectively, and were built until 1954. This
powerful, smooth six-cylinder 40 horsepower
Row Crop 77 was typical of the new Fleetlines,
and boasted the new Hydra-Lectric hydraulics
system beginning in 1949.

Chapter 9

The Orphan Tractors

Tractors of Many Colors

Tractor historians have traced the lineage of more than 1,000 different American and Canadian tractor manufacturers that built at least one model.

Many of these "manufacturers" were blacksmiths that created a one-off tractor or small ventures that built a prototype that never made it into series production; others built a range of models over several decades before being chased out of business by the giant corporations.

These once-upon-a-time tractor makers are collectively known as the orphan brands.

Among the numerous brands of orphan tractors were many creative, even revolutionary, ideas—as well as just oddball inventions. Consider the Hackney Auto Plow, made in St. Paul, Minnesota, in the 1910s, which was basically an automobile fitted with an undercarriage plow. Or the Chase Motor Truck from Syracuse, New York, which ran on three rolling drums and was termed a tractor-roller.

And there was also the Happy Farmer tractor from Minneapolis, the crawler Auto-Track-Tractor from San Francisco designed to run in the moist soil of the California valleys, and many more. The history of these orphan tractors was as varied as the colors they were painted.

Opposite page
Eagle 20-35 Model E
The Eagle Manufacturing Company of Appleton, Wisconsin, first entered the farm equipment market in 1906 with a 32 horsepower tractor. They returned to the marketplace several years later, in 1929 offering this 20-35 Model E. Based on a two-cylinder traction engine design, the engine measured 8.00x9.00in bore and stroke. A truly massive affair, it was rated at 20 drawbar horsepower and 35 belt-pulley horsepower. This Model E has been owned for the last thirty-five years by Clayton Badglay of Kinde, Michigan.

Farm Motors Tilsoil 18-30

The Farm Motors Company of Canada built its massive Tilsoil 18-30 tractor in 1922. The engine had a 7.00in bore and 8.00in stroke and reached a maximum engine operating speed of 700rpm, enough to push the Tilsoil to a 3.25mph top speed. Only about 300 of these monstrous 6,300 pound tractors were ever built.

Left

Eagle 20-40 Model H

The Eagle Manufacturing Company built its Model H alongside the Model E from 1926–1938. With an identical 8.00in bore to the Model E, but a 1.00in longer stroke at 10.00in, the Model H created a brawny 40 horsepower at the drawbar. Eagle built tractors from 1906, but halted production during World War II never to start its assembly lines again.

Previous pages

Robert Bell Imperial Super-Drive

The famous Canadian Robert Bell Engine & Thresher Company of Seaforth, Ontario, was a successful builder of a range of threshing machines. Robert Bell also sold a line of farm tractors in the 1920s, including this Imperial Super-Drive. The Imperial was actually built by the Illinois Tractor Company of Bloomington, Illinois, and sold under Bell's name in Canada. This Imperial Super-Drive was photographed at the Ontario Agricultural Museum show, The Great Canadian Field Days, in Milton, Ontario.

Gray-Dort

The Gray-Dort was not an actual farm tractor but a converted automobile, a popular modification with down-and-out farmers during the Great Depression of the 1930s.

Right

Gray-Dort

This 1920 Gray-Dort was built as a joint venture by the Gray Sons Campbell of Chatham, Canada, and the Dort Motor Company of Detroit. Interesting features are the 20in truck rims on mower wheels and the Chevrolet steering. This rare bit of history is owned by Rick Guy of Ontario, Canada.

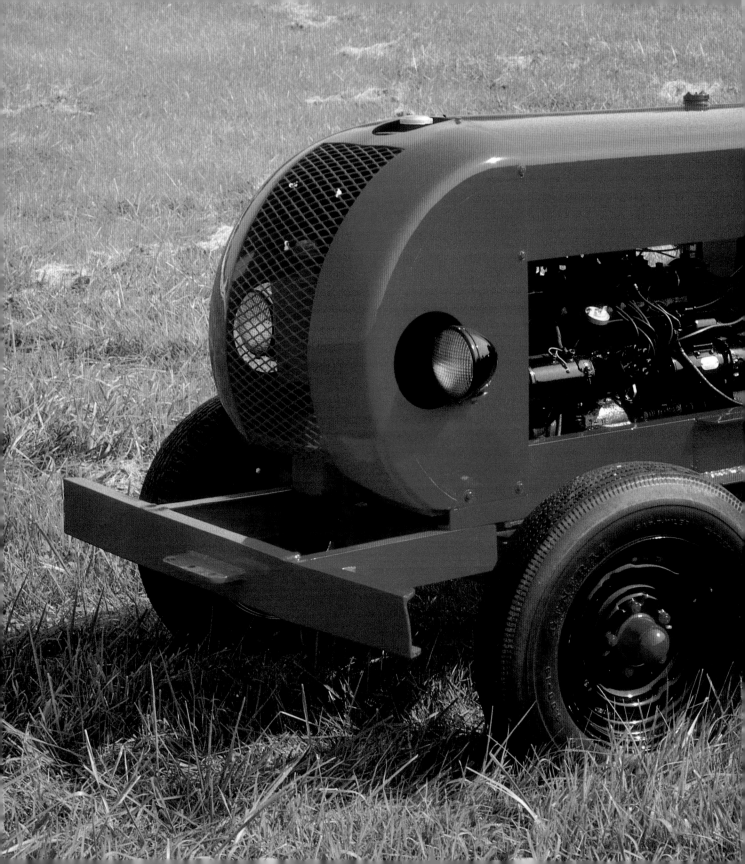

Friday Model 048

This 1949 Model 048 had a six-cylinder Chrysler Industrial 90 horsepower engine backed by a Dodge five-speed gearbox and a two-speed rear axle. Top speed was about 60mph, making the Friday ideal for hauling produce to market. This Friday Model 048 is owned by Larry Darling of Hartford, Michigan, where the tractors were once built.

Previous pages
Friday Model 048

The Friday Tractor Company of Hartford, Michigan, first offered its Model 048 in about 1948. The Friday was designed specifically for orchard use and for delivering produce to market. The Friday line was offered into the late 1950s.

Duplex Co-op No. 2

The Duplex Machinery Company of Battle Creek, Michigan, introduced its No. 1 tractor in 1937. The No. 1 was followed by the No. 2; this No. 2 was built in 1938, and bears serial number 1165. In mid-1938, Duplex Machinery changed its name to the Co-operative Manufacturing Company.

Right
Duplex Co-op No. 2

The top-of-the-range Co-op No. 2 was powered by the smooth, powerful six-cylinder Chrysler engine, which gave a reputed top speed of 28mph. This rare tractor is owned by Ivan Henderson of Hutchinson, Ontario, Canada.

B. F. Avery Model A

The B. F. Avery Company of Louisville, Kentucky, is not to be confused with the larger, more-productive, and longer-lived Avery Company of Peoria, Illinois. B. F. Avery produced only a handful of models through its short history, including this Model A, 22 horsepower general-purpose tractor.

Right

B. F. Avery Model A

The Model A was a Cletrac General row-crop tractor built by B. F. Avery because the Cleveland Tractor Company wanted to concentrate on crawler tractors. The 2,725 pound Model A was powered by a four-cylinder Hercules engine of 133ci. The engine featured a bore of 3.25in and a stroke of 4.00in with an engine-operating range of 1200–1800rpm, all of which made the Model A a useful row-crop tractor. B. F. Avery built the model A beginning in 1941.

Waterloo Bronco

The Bronco was powered by the 12 horsepower Wisconsin two-cylinder, air-cooled TE engine. The bore was a full 3.00in and the stroke measured 3.25in. Top speed was 8mph with three forward gears and one reverse. This rare Canadian specialty is owned by Keith Johnston of Kitchener, Ontario, Canada.

Left
Waterloo Bronco

The Waterloo Company of Ontario, Canada, offered its Bronco row-crop tractor between the years 1948 and 1950, though only about 1,000 were ever built. This firm is not to be confused with other tractor makes using the name Waterloo in their titles, including the Waterloo Gasoline Engine Company of Waterloo, Iowa, builders of the famous Waterloo Boy.

Previous pages
Leader Model D

The Leader Tractor Manufacturing Company of Chagrin Falls, Ohio, first offered its Model D tractor in the late 1940s. Note the odd but effective square-shaped rear wheels. This 2,500 pound tractor was powered by a four-cylinder Hercules 1XB-5 engine of 133ci. Rated at 22 horsepower, the Model D was an ideal row-crop and truck farming tractor for the small farmer. This rare Model D was built in 1948 and is owned by Bill Kuhn of Kinde, Michigan.

Index